Big Panda
and
Tiny Dragon

Big Panda
and
Tiny Dragon

James Norbury

Michael Joseph
an imprint of
Penguin Books

This book is dedicated
to everyone who gets lost.

Contents

Spring

Be brave.

You never know what a
first meeting might lead to.

'A new day and a new beginning,'
said Tiny Dragon.

'What shall we do with it?'

'Which is more important,' asked Big Panda,
'the journey or the destination?'

'The company,' said Tiny Dragon.

'I'm too busy to see the flowers right now,' said Tiny Dragon.

'All the more reason to look at them,' said Big Panda.
'And they might not be here tomorrow.'

'Isn't nature incredible!' said Tiny Dragon.

'It is,' agreed Big Panda.
'But we are just as much a part of nature
as the tree or the spider, and just as amazing.'

'Big Panda,' said Tiny Dragon,
'I like the way you listen to me
and talk to me and travel with me,
but most of all, I like the way
you make me feel.'

'Try to make time for the small things,'
said Big Panda.

'They are often the most important.'

'The most important thing . . .'
said Big Panda,

'. . . is to pay attention.'

'Just because you don't know where you
are going, it doesn't mean you are lost,'
said Tiny Dragon profoundly.

'Very true,' replied Big Panda,
'but in this case we are definitely lost.'

'That tree has been through some rough times,'
said Tiny Dragon.

'Yes,' said Big Panda, 'but it's still here
and it has gained strength and beauty.'

'Hurry!' squeaked Tiny Dragon.
'There is so much to do!'

'The river doesn't hurry,' said Big Panda,
'yet despite many obstacles,
always gets where it's going.'

'Nothing is happening,' said Tiny Dragon.

'Maybe,' said Big Panda,
'it's happening underneath first.'

'Sometimes I think I'm not good enough,'
said Tiny Dragon.

'A cherry tree doesn't compare itself
to other trees,' said Big Panda,
'it just blossoms.'

Uses for a leaf: no. 1 – a boat.

'Sometimes, you just have to be silly.'

Each decision you make on your
journey takes you closer or further
from where you want to go.

'Mistakes mean you're trying,' said Big Panda.
'Don't give up.'

'I want to change the world,' said Tiny Dragon.

'Start with the next person who needs your help,' replied Big Panda.

'The map doesn't show
where I'm supposed to go,'
said Tiny Dragon.

'Your journey isn't shown
on any map,' said Big Panda.
'You must discover your own path.'

'I miss him already,' said Tiny Dragon.
'What if he gets hurt?'

'You helped him when he needed it most,'
said Big Panda,
'and what if he goes on to live a long
and happy life?'

'The path ahead looks difficult,' said Big Panda.

'No matter how hard it gets,' said Tiny Dragon,
'we'll face it together.'

'I wish this moment could last for ever,'
said Tiny Dragon.

'This moment is all there is,'
smiled Big Panda.

Summer

Time doing nothing is never wasted.

'I wish I had met you earlier,'
said Tiny Dragon, 'so we could have gone
on even more adventures together.'

'What is my purpose?' asked Tiny Dragon.

Big Panda paused, then said,
'To sit on that stone and be with your friend.'

'My head feels like this storm sometimes,'
said Tiny Dragon.

'If you really listen,' said Big Panda,
'you can hear the raindrops
splashing on the stone.
It's possible to find a little peace,
even in a storm.'

An Elder Dragon
is a Tiny Dragon
who never gave up.

GRANDPA DRAGON

'We have a long way to go,' said Big Panda.

Tiny Dragon grinned. 'Grandpa Dragon used to say,
"A journey of a thousand miles begins with a cup of tea."'

'You're a good listener,' said Tiny Dragon.

'Listening has never landed me in trouble,'
replied Big Panda.

'I can't find the right place for this last branch,'
huffed Tiny Dragon.

Big Panda chewed his bamboo thoughtfully.
'It's the imperfections that make it perfect.'

'The best thing to have with tea,'
said Big Panda, 'is a good friend.'

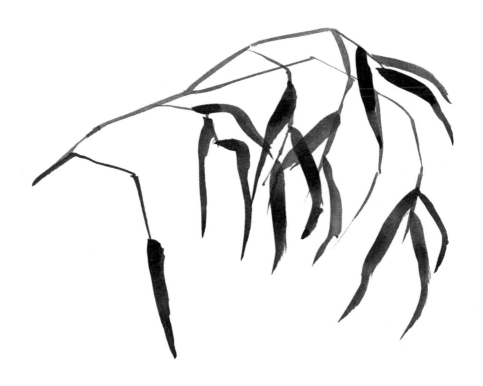

'I'm worried,' said Tiny Dragon.
'I don't know what to do next.'

'For just a moment,' said Big Panda,
'stop, breathe and listen to
the wind in the bamboo.'

'What are you doing?'
asked Tiny Dragon.

'I've no idea,' said Big Panda,
'but it's great fun.'

If you seek happiness for others,
you may find it for yourself.

'You know,' said Tiny Dragon,
'these might be the good old days that
we'll look back on with great longing.'

'In that case,' said Big Panda,
'let's never stop making them.'

Love needs no explanation.

Together, we can do anything.

Some people are like candles.

They burn themselves out
to create light for others.

Uses for a leaf: no. 17 – a parasol (and dinner).

'Hurry up, Big Panda,
we're going to be late!'

Big Panda sat down.
'I like to think I'm creating anticipation.'

'This garden is beautiful,' said Tiny Dragon.

Big Panda nodded. 'And we only found it
because we went the wrong way so many times.'

'You don't do much,'
said Tiny Dragon.

'I'm full of potential,'
yawned Big Panda.

Autumn

'Autumn is here,' said Big Panda,
'and soon winter will be upon us.'

'Oooh . . .' said Tiny Dragon.
'More cosy evenings together . . . with tea.'

Uses for a leaf: no. 62 – an umbrella.

'We're lost again,' said Big Panda.

'When I'm lost,' said Tiny Dragon,
'I find it helps to go back to the beginning
and try to remember why I started.'

'What if I meet people who don't like me
or the things I do?' asked Tiny Dragon.

'You must walk your own path,' said Big Panda.
'Better to lose them than lose yourself.'

86   autumn

'My flower . . .' said Tiny Dragon.

'All things must come to pass, little one.
That's what makes them so precious.'

'It's hard being kind to everyone,' said Tiny Dragon.

'True,' said Big Panda, 'and hardest of all to be kind to ourselves, but we must try.'

Let go or be dragged.

When drinking tea . . . drink tea.

'What are you thinking about?'
asked Tiny Dragon.

'Nothing,' said Big Panda.
'It's wonderful.'

'I can't find my way out of this hole,'
said Tiny Dragon.

Big Panda smiled.
'Then I will come and sit in it with you.'

'The leaves are dying,' said Tiny Dragon.

'Don't be sad,' said Big Panda.
'Autumn is nature's way of showing
us how beautiful letting go can be.'

'Look what I found.'

'Oh,' said Big Panda,
'an opportunity to try something new.'

'You're quiet today,' said Tiny Dragon.

Big Panda smiled.
'I don't think I can improve on the sound of the rain.'

'I'm not sure this is working . . .'

'How is that tree still standing?' asked Tiny Dragon.

'During better times,' said Big Panda, 'it grew deep roots.
Now it can weather any storm.'

'It's a shame we didn't plant this tree a long time ago,'
said Tiny Dragon. 'Imagine how big it would be.'

'We're doing it now,' said Big Panda.
'That's the important thing.'

'Can you hear the wind in the trees, Tiny Dragon?

That's nature's way of telling us to take a moment
to stop, breathe and just be.'

'Are you ever mean to yourself, Big Panda?'

Big Panda watched the ripples spread across the lake.

'I see how gentle you are, Tiny Dragon,
and try to treat myself with the same kindness.'

'There have been so many difficulties along this path,'
said Tiny Dragon.

'There have,' agreed Big Panda, 'but we have
learned something from each one.

And imagine how good the view
will be when we reach the top.'

'Whether people praise you
or criticize you, Tiny Dragon,
try to accept it gracefully.

It takes all kinds of conditions
to create a strong tree.'

Listening to someone is one of the
greatest things you can do for them.

When you light a lantern
for someone else,
you cannot help but
light up your own path.

'If you don't try,' said Big Panda,
'you'll never know if you can fly.'

'I'm tired,' sighed Tiny Dragon.

'Then it's time to stop,' said Big Panda,
'watch the stars and have a cup of hot tea.'

'What are you celebrating?' asked Tiny Dragon.

'Getting rained on,' said Big Panda. 'With you.'

'That's a very small candle,' said Tiny Dragon.

'However small the light,' smiled Big Panda,
'it's better than darkness.'

'I want to open a scary pumpkin stall,'
said Tiny Dragon, 'but I'm afraid I'll fail.'

Big Panda poured his friend some more tea.

'You might fail, little one, but if you let fear stop
you from even trying, failure is assured.'

Sometimes all you can do
is make someone a cup of tea.

It might be enough.

There are days
when just getting up is a victory.

'What is the Universe?' asked Tiny Dragon.

Big Panda looked up at the night sky.

'We are, little one. We are depthless oceans and summer
lightning – there is nothing more magnificent.'

Winter

'You've been carrying me for so many days now,'
said Tiny Dragon.

'It could be worse,' said Big Panda.
'We could be Big Dragon and Tiny Panda.'

'Each season is completely different,' said Big Panda,
'yet each has its wonders.'

'Just like us,' grinned Tiny Dragon.

Sometimes, it's good to head out
with no idea where you're going.

'How do you keep going?'
asked Tiny Dragon.

'Sometimes,' said Big Panda,
'even the smallest step
is better than no step.'

'It's the shortest day,' said Tiny Dragon.
'Winter is truly upon us.'

'But also the longest night,' said Big Panda
'and that comes with its own wonders.'

'I give up,' said Tiny Dragon.

'That's OK,' said Big Panda.
'We'll try again tomorrow.'

'It's cold and dark tonight,' said Tiny Dragon.

'Don't worry, little one,' said Big Panda.
'The sun will rise again.'

'If you're struggling, little one, you can tell me.

I want to help.'

'Do bad thoughts make me a bad person?' asked Tiny Dragon.

'No,' said Big Panda. 'The waves are not the ocean.
The thoughts are not the mind.'

'I am so tired,' said Tiny Dragon.

Big Panda paused. 'Winter is a time when nature withdraws, rests and gathers its energy for a new beginning.

We are allowed to do the same, my little friend.'

'I forgot to make my New Year's resolution,'
sighed Tiny Dragon.

'Don't worry, little one,' said Big Panda.
'If there's something you want to change
you can start right now.'

'What would your three wishes be?'
asked Tiny Dragon.

Big Panda pondered a moment.
'Us together . . . travelling . . . in the rain.'

'There is beauty everywhere,' said Big Panda,
'but sometimes it's difficult to see.'

Uses for a leaf: no. 111 – a sledge.

'I can't explain how I feel,'
said Tiny Dragon.

Big Panda smiled. 'That's OK.
Words are not adequate for all things.'

You give me strength when all mine has gone.

Spring

Butterflies struggle most just before they emerge.

'Do you believe in reincarnation?'
asked Tiny Dragon.

Big Panda yawned. 'I believe that
every minute of every day,
we can let go and start again.'

Even a damaged tree can produce
the most beautiful blossoms.

'Are we nearly there yet?'
asked Tiny Dragon.

Big Panda smiled.
'I hope not.'

Afterword

Some time ago, while I was in a difficult place, I happened across a book on Buddhism in a second-hand bookshop. I found the content fascinating and began investigating spirituality and meditation in greater depth. The more I learned, the more I realized I didn't need to be a slave to my negative thoughts.

Having discovered something that so improved my happiness, I became more determined to help others. I joined the Samaritans, taking calls from people reaching out for help with loneliness, anxiety and depression. The amount of human suffering really shocked me and inspired me to start a small support group for my local area, but the arrival of COVID put a stop to those plans.

Instead, I decided to draw pictures as a way of communicating these powerful, transformational ideas to people in simple, accessible ways. Initially, I had no idea how successful it would be, but I've been contacted by people from many different cultures, religions, countries and age groups letting me know how much my pictures have helped them through difficult times.

I put all my heart into each picture and I think that's why they speak to people – each and every one has a little piece of my soul in it.

Acknowledgements

This book is the culmination of a lifetime's experience. I therefore acknowledge everyone I've ever met; you have all forged me into the person I am now, and if I were not that person, I could not have created this – so thank you.

But some people really stand out as having made this book a reality.

Ruth, who has always helped me just by being herself. She's the centre of my world and I love her more each day.

My mother and father, who taught me to be self-reliant, to value art as a way to convey ideas and who supported me with all my strange plans. Without them in my life, I would have never believed it possible to make a living from art – thank you.

My brother and sister Alan and Jayne – you're always so encouraging and supporting.

Ludo, I can't believe you did it. I wrote to so many agents, and you are the only one who believed in me. Thank you so much. I hope your faith is rewarded. I like to think I have gained a friend and an agent. And Eve, I know how much you do behind the scenes – thank you.

Dan, I really lucked out with you. I could not imagine any other editor having shared my vision so strongly or understood so deeply what I was trying to do. And many thanks to everyone else at Penguin who has worked so hard to bring my funny little pictures to the world – Aggie, Bea, Sarah, Lee, Jon, Tracy, Dan P-B, Rebecca, Anjali, Vanessa, Sophie, Ellie and Christina.

My followers on social media, without your support and encouragement I would not have carried on. Thank you.

My fellow Samaritans, it can be rough sometimes; knowing we are all there for each other makes a huge difference. Talking on the phone with the callers is a privilege and their words have changed me in ways I can't explain. I don't think this book would exist without them.

And of course my animal friends – you keep me sane while driving me insane.

MICHAEL JOSEPH

UK | USA | Canada | Ireland | Australia
India | New Zealand | South Africa

Michael Joseph is part of the Penguin
Random House group of companies
whose addresses can be found at
global.penguinrandomhouse.com.

Penguin
Random House
UK

First published in Great Britain by
Michael Joseph, 2021
013

Text copyright © James Norbury, 2021
Illustration copyright © James Norbury, 2021

The moral right of the author has been
asserted

Set in Bellefair

Colour origination by Altaimage, London
Printed and bound in the UK by TJ Books Ltd

A CIP catalogue record for this book is
available from the British Library

ISBN: 978–0–241–52932–4

www.greenpenguin.co.uk

MIX
Paper from
responsible sources
FSC® C018179
www.fsc.org

Penguin Random House is committed to a
sustainable future for our business, our readers
and our planet. This book is made from Forest
Stewardship Council® certified paper.